The Meaning and Measurement of Moral Development

by Lawrence Kohlberg

Clark University Press
Worcester, Massachusetts 1981

Copyright 1981 by Clark University Press

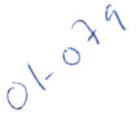

Library of Congress Cataloging in Publication Data
Kohlberg, Lawrence, 1927-
  The meaning and measurement of moral development
  (Heinz Werner lectures ; v. 13 (1979))
  Bibliography: p.
  1. Moral development. 2. Moral development—
Testing. 1. Title. II. Series.
BF723.M54K63   155.4'18   80-70800
ISBN 0-914206-18-4   AACR2

THE MEANING AND MEASUREMENT OF MORAL DEVELOPMENT

Drawing by Leonard Baskin

THE HEINZ WERNER LECTURES

Ludwig von Bertalanffy
Organismic Psychology and Systems Theory, 1966

Jean Piaget
On the Development of Memory and Identity, 1967

Jerome S. Bruner
Processes of Cognitive Growth, 1968

Roman Jakobson
The Paths from Infancy to Language, 1969

Conrad H. Waddington
Biology, Purpose and Ethics, 1970

Kenneth Burke
Dramatism and Development, 1971

Rene Dubos
Of Human Diversity, 1972

Errol E. Harris
Perceptual Assurance and the Reality of the World, 1973

Bernard Kaplan
Rationality and Irrationality in Development, 1974

J. McVicker Hunt
Early Psychological Development and Experience, 1976

Herman A. Witkin
Cognitive Styles in Personal and Cultural Adaptation, 1977

Jane Loevinger
Scientific Ways in the Study of Ego Development, 1978

Lawrence Kohlberg
The Meaning and Measurement of Moral Development, 1979

THE HEINZ WERNER LECTURES

Ludwig von Bertalanffy
Organismic Psychology and Systems Theory, 1966

Jean Piaget
On the Development of Memory and Identity, 1967

Jerome S. Bruner
Processes of Cognitive Growth, 1968

Roman Jakobson
The Paths from Infancy to Language, 1969

Conrad H. Waddington
Biology, Purpose and Ethics, 1970

Kenneth Burke
Dramatism and Development, 1971

Rene Dubos
Of Human Diversity, 1972

Errol E. Harris
Perceptual Assurance and the Reality of the World, 1973

Bernard Kaplan
Rationality and Irrationality in Development, 1974

J. McVicker Hunt
Early Psychological Development and Experience, 1976

Herman A. Witkin
Cognitive Styles in Personal and Cultural Adaptation, 1977

Jane Loevinger
Scientific Ways in the Study of Ego Development, 1978

Lawrence Kohlberg
The Meaning and Measurement of Moral Development, 1979

CONTENTS

ONE/THE MEANING AND MEASUREMENT
OF MORAL DEVELOPMENT 1

    Assumptions Concerning Personality and
    Development: Divergences 4

    On Test Construction and Test Scoring:
    Shared Assumptions 7

    On Test Construction and Test Scoring:
    Divergent Assumptions 9

    Illustrations of Test Construction and
    Test Scoring (Loevinger vs. Kohlberg) 9

TWO/EXPLORING THE MORAL ATMOSPHERE OF
INSTITUTIONS: A BRIDGE BETWEEN MORAL
JUDGMENT AND MORAL ACTION 35

REFERENCES 53

ONE

The Meaning and Measurement of Moral Development

The title of this first lecture consciously evokes the work of Jane Loevinger (1966) on the meaning and measurement of ego development, reported in her Heinz Werner memorial lecture of last year (Loevinger, 1979). In reporting the work that I have done in recent years with Anne Colby and John Gibbs (1978) on the measurement of moral development, I will compare assumptions and results with those of Loevinger, indicating the assumptions which we share and the assumptions on which we diverge. The central theme of my comparison with Loevinger is that developmental tests, tests assuming qualitatively different types of response ordered in an invariant sequence, presuppose different theoretical and methodological assumptions about personality and its assessment than do psychometric tests or traditional personality tests.

Before engaging these issues, we need to ask whether we should try to make stage-developmental tests at all. Piaget and many Piagetians rejected the idea of constructing a stage test, relying instead upon a clinical interview, theoretically interpreted and used to examine hypotheses derived from Piagetian stage theory. When I started work in the area, reported in my 1958 dissertation (Kohlberg, 1958), I did not think that my clinically probed interviews about hypothetical dilemmas constituted a test, nor that I should aim in that direction. I thought I was operating in the tradition of Henry Murray, who got numbers for research exploration by asking for clinical ratings of TAT's or other open-ended material. If there was reasonable agreement among raters in assigning numbers, and if the numbers yielded theoretically meaningful results, that was sufficient warrant for the method. I called my 1958 dissertation method a rating system for assessing developmental ideal types.

When Kurtines and Grief (1974) criticized this 1958 method for failing to meet psychometric criteria for a test, including test-retest reliability, I was extremely surprised since I had never claimed that the method was a test.

Somewhat before the Kurtines and Grief article appeared, both Jim Rest and I had decided that one or more tests of moral stage development were required. After our exploratory work which yielded clinical definitions of stages, we entered a second phase of research which required a more reliable and valid assessment method, that is, a test. The first and most obvious consideration was that starting with the work of Moshe Blatt (Blatt & Kohlberg, 1975) we had become involved in work in moral education, which requires a test for evaluation or interpretation of experimental change.

A more basic reason was that revision, refinement, or even rejection of our moral stage theory rested on developing a reliable and valid method of assigning individuals to a stage. This became apparent to me in reflecting upon the problem of apparent "regression" in moral stage in the college years (Kohlberg & Kramer, 1969; Kohlberg, 1973). Using the 1958 dissertation method, Kramer found that almost 25% of our longitudinal cases "regressed" or dropped in stage in late adolescence. We could have interpreted these cases as casting doubt on our method, as an indication that our assessment method had low reliability or validity. Instead, Kramer and I concluded that many of the anomalies represented genuine retrogression, which a theory of invariant stage response had to address, rather than being method error. Further reflection led me to reassert our belief in the theoretical postulate of invariant sequence and to interpret the anomalies not as retrogression but as representing weakness in our clinical method's ability to handle subjects who were in transitional states. Rather than retrogressing from Stage 4 social morality to Stage 2 instrumental egoism, many of our anomalous cases should be considered Stage 4½, a highly relativistic transitional level between conventional and principled moral judgment. Their skepticism, conflict, and questioning about the stage they had been in, Stage 4, was the dominant feature of their response, and the reasoning was only superficially like Stage 2. It was in fact a step out of Stage

4, and further longitudinal observation suggested that it was eventually a step into Stage 5. Such alternations, between revision and doubt about the theory and revision and doubt about the method, clearly indicated the need to develop a more precise or reliable stage-scoring system. In work prior to 1969, we had claimed substantial support for moral stage theory based on results with groups, cross-sectional age data in a variety of cultures. The real data required for testing and revising stage theory, however, was not group data but individual longitudinal data. In a 1969 article I said: "While the group data indicate a hierarchy of difficulty or advance in our moral types, they do not demonstrate an invariant sequence of stages. This can be done only by following individuals longitudinally through the sequence" (Kohlberg, 1969, p. 386). Following individuals longitudinally through the sequence requires a method with a minimum of measurement error and for that reason implies the need for a reliable and valid assignment of a stage score to an individual interview, in other words, a test.

I have explained how my theoretical concerns and clinical assessments led me after over ten years of research to construct a test. Jane Loevinger's movement has been in the reverse direction, from an early concern for developing a test of personality or ego to theoretical statements such as her recent book, *Ego Development* (Loevinger, 1976). In comparing the views of Loevinger and myself, I shall first consider the topic of theoretical assumptions about personality development and morality. Next, I'll consider assumptions of test construction and classification of responses. Finally, I shall consider the topic of the reliability and validity of the test, once constructed.

With regard to each topic, I shall first review the assumptions I share with Loevinger, then our divergences.

The first shared assumption is the assumption of ego, that there is a relatively unitary, conscious part of the personality, the ego or self, which reasons, judges, or evaluates. The second shared assumption is the assumption of stages. These stages form: (1) an invariant sequence of (2) hierarchical transformations, which are (3) structured wholes. Both Loevinger and I, then, accept the applicability of Piaget's hierarchical stage model to the characterization of ego development. In addition, we both accept the idea that moral judgment, reasoning, and character is one major part, aspect, or domain of ego development, relating to a more general ego stage. Third, there are striking parallels in the stage descriptions which emerge from Loevinger's writings and mine. This parallelism is empirical as well as conceptual. Lambert (1972) and Sullivan, McCullough, and Stager (1964) find significant correlations between the Loevinger test of ego development and our moral stage assessments after age and IQ are partialled out.

Assumptions Concerning Personality and Development: Divergences

While Loevinger does seem to get her conception of hierarchical stages from Piaget, her dominant orientation is primarily to neo-psychoanalytic conceptions of ego development (see Table 1). In contradistinction, I orient not to psychodynamic theory but to the cognitive-developmental theories of moralization: to that of Piaget (1932) and of the American forerunners of Piaget — James Mark Baldwin (1897), John Dewey (1932), and George Herbert Mead (1934). The difference in theoretical orientation leads to at least four differences in the nature of the development we seek to assess or measure.

First, there are differences between us on how to define stages and articulate their inner logic. Loevinger defines her stages partly in terms of structures, partly in terms of functions and motives pertaining to self-enhancement and defense. I define stages solely in terms of cognitive structures, or ways of thinking or judging. Our different theoretical orientations, then, lead to differences in the formulation of a "stage," and hence to differences in what we are trying to measure. We both seek to measure thought and judgment structures used by the ego; Loevinger tries to measure ego functions and motives as well.

Second, there are differences between us in dividing the domain of ego development. Loevinger posits a single differentiated but yet indivisible ego simultaneously engaged in cognitive, interpersonal, and moral functioning. From Loevinger's point of view, there is no need to divide the ego domain. In our view, the ego comprises relatively circumscribed and self-contained subdomains, each possessed of a distinct structure,

TABLE 1: **The Loevinger and Kohlberg Stages Compared**
(Ego Stage Types of Sullivan, Grant, & Grant; Peck; Kohlberg; Bull; and Perry are from Loevinger, 1976)

APPROXIMATE EGO LEVEL	SULLIVAN, GRANT, AND GRANT LEVELS OF INTEGRATION	PECK CHARACTER TYPE	KOHLBERG BASIS FOR MORALITY	BULL TYPE OF MORALITY	PERRY INTELLECTUAL-ETHICAL PARADIGM
Presocial					
Impulsive	1. Separateness	Amoral	Punishment and obedience	Anomy	
Self-Protective	2. Non-self differences	Expedient	Naive instrumental hedonism	Heteronomy	Duality
Conformist	3. Rules ("Cons")	Conformist	Good relations and approval	Socionomy	Multiplicity prelegitimate
	3. Rules (Conformists)				Multiplicity
Conscientious-Conformist	4. Conflict and response		Law and order		
Conscientious		Irrational-conscientious	Democratic contract	Autonomy	Relativism
Individualistic	5. Continuity	Rational-altruistic	Individual principles of conscience		
Autonomous	6. Self-consistency				
Integrated	7. Relativity				Commitment

regardless of the functioning of a unitary ego. Whereas Loevinger seeks to capture in her ego stages the interpenetration of ego development, cognitive style, self concerns, and moral or character development, we take these different aspects of functioning as governed by different cognitive structures. Thus cognitive style, for us, points to the domain of structure defined by Piaget's stages of cognitive or logical operations. Interpersonal style and self concerns point, for us, to the domain of structure studied by Selman in his attempt to delineate the stages of role taking, social perspective, and concepts of interpersonal relations (Selman & Jaquette, 1977). Impulse control and character terms denote, to us, the domain of structure called moral judgment and reasoning. We attempt to assess only this latter domain —the development of moral judgment.

On the basis of Piagetian theory, as modified under the impact of empirical findings (cf. Kohlberg, 1976), I have been led to hypothesize parallel and corresponding stages in each ego domain, and also to argue that attainment of a stage in any one domain is dependent on attainment of a certain stage in one of the other domains. Thus, I assume that attainment of Piaget's stage of formal cognitive operations is a necessary but not sufficient condition for the attainment of Selman's fourth stage of interpersonal conceptions. This stage requires taking a third-person perspective on dyadic relations, conceptions of responsibility in relationships, and social achievement. In turn, I assume that Selman's fourth stage of social cognition must be attained in order for our fourth stage of moral judgment to be achieved, that is, for the emergence of concepts of duty defined by conscience and by the underlying values and laws of the individual's society. Here again, it is a question of a necessary but not a sufficient condition. The notion of necessary but not sufficient conditions includes our notion of the meaning of moral judgment stage for motivation and behavior. What we conceptualize as moral reasoning is a cognitive competence, necessary but not sufficient for given kinds of motivation and conduct.

In summary, then, Loevinger defines and seeks to assess a unitary ego which uses various structures or competencies but which is a concrete unity of function reflected in motive and action. We claim less: only parallelisms in thought structure which are necessary but not sufficient for given kinds of action.

Third, and in part derived from the first two, there are differences between Loevinger and myself about what we are trying to measure. Loevinger, it would seem, was not oriented toward constructing a test useful for educational and experimental change studies, although her test has been used for this purpose more recently. I wanted to construct a test that would not only assess the current stage of moral functioning and would validly and reliably assess stage change, but also one that would reflect my concern with educational goals and my belief that a higher stage is a better stage. In other words, I include in my approach a normative component which Loevinger does not.

Fourthly, then, this normative concern has led me to rely upon philosophic as well as psychological theory in defining what I study. That is, I assumed the need to define philosophically the entity we study, moral judgment, and to give a philosophic rationale for why a higher stage is a better stage. My philosophic conception of moral judgment has been based on principles of justice and has depended upon the theories of Kant and of Rawls (1971) to justify the principles of the highest stages.

Having discussed the commonalities and differences between Loevinger and myself with regard to theoretical issues, let me turn now to the assumptions, shared and divergent, with respect to test construction and test scoring.

On Test Construction and Test Scoring: Shared Assumptions

A traditional psychometrician, in scoring, let us say, the Binet test, is concerned solely with whether a given response is "right" or "wrong" as defined by the content of the response. The manner in which an individual arrives at the response is irrelevant. The psychometrician's act of scoring is then, in essence, no different from that which is found in machine scoring. The scorer need have no knowledge of theory, and is, indeed, precluded from making a clinical interpretation in the light of theory.

In contrast, one who seeks to locate responses with regard to underlying structure makes a distinction between "achievement" and "process," to use Heinz Werner's formulation: a distinction between the correctness of the response according to some standard of correctness and the ways of arriving at the response. In order to arrive at the underlying structure of a response, one must construct a test, for example, the Pinard-Laurendeau scale, so that the questions and the responses to them allow for an unambiguous inference to be drawn as to underlying structure. The stage of causal reasoning, moral reasoning, and so on, at which an individual is functioning cannot be arrived at here merely by correlating manifest similarities and differences in the content or "correctness" of responses. Instead, this test constructor must postulate structure from the start, as opposed to inductively finding structure in content after the test is made. Thus, the kind of structure to which we refer is not that derived from the factor analysis of psychometric tests, exemplified in the work of Thurstone and Guilford. If a test is to yield *stage* structure, a concept of that structure must be built into the initial act of observation, test construction, and scoring; it will not emerge through pure factor-analytic responses classified by content.

Both Loevinger, who comes from a psychometric background, and I, whose testing of subjects has been governed by Piagetian assumptions, move away from the traditional psychometric procedures. A first point of agreement, therefore, is that we both are trying to construct tests which will tap underlying structures. We also agree that the test constructor finds developmental structure not by the inductive method but by an abductive method which involves a working back and forth, or mutual bootstrapping, between theoretical assumptions such as postulated structures on the one hand, and empirical reflections of those structures in the responses subjects give, on the other.

A further point of agreement is that the test scorer as well as the test constructor must know the underlying theory, and also function as a "clinician" who can infer structures from the content in responses. The test scorer must function in a quasi-clinical manner, going from a response to postulated underlying structures, and then testing the inference to particular structures by looking at additional response material.

On Test Construction and Test Scoring: Divergent Assumptions

Of greater interest and significance are those issues with regard to which Loevinger and I diverge. As I have just done with regard to the shared assumptions, I shall summarize these briefly with minimal comment. I shall then use an item on my test and an item on Loevinger's test in order to show more concretely what each of us takes into account in constructing the items, scoring the items, or both. My hope is that this examination will flesh out our divergent assumptions, and clarify our differences in "arriving at structure."

There are three basic ways in which Loevinger and I are in disagreement with regard to test construction and test scoring. (1) Loevinger does not oppose content and structure — I do. (2) Loevinger constructs and scores her items so as to be able to infer a hypothetical entity, a kind of underlying structure akin to the psychoanalytic ego. The structures we seek to tap in test construction and arrive at in test scoring are abstractable from responses as their form or quality. (3) Leovinger makes use of a "sign approach," one which combines empirical probabilities with theoretical considerations in a bootstrapping process which she calls "saving circularity." My colleagues and I reject the "sign approach," and have required each item in the manual to clearly reflect the structure of the stage to which it is keyed.

Illustrations of Test Construction and Test Scoring (Loevinger vs. Kohlberg)

All of this, of course, is quite abstract and condensed. I therefore turn now to the illustrative material so that we may better see how Loevinger and I relate to each other on matters of testing.

My test, as some of you know, consists of two forms — A and B. Each form includes three hypothetical moral dilemmas: one exhibiting a conflict between helping someone to enhance the quality of life, in violation of the law, versus obedience to the law; a second dealing with conflict between regard for character and conscience versus the meting out of retributive justice or punishment and deterrence; the third involving a conflict between the maintenance of a contract as opposed to the upholding of legitimate authority. Thus, in one of the dilemmas, subjects are asked whether a doctor should give an overdose of morphine to a terminal cancer patient if she requests it. This dilemma is the counterpart on Form B to the better known Heinz dilemma, which deals with whether a husband should steal a drug to save his wife's life. In both instances, the dilemma pertains to the moral conflict between quality of life at the expense of law and obedience to law at the sacrifice of quality of life. Taking the construction of this Form B dilemma and the scoring of responses to it as paradigmatic, I shall try to show how we put structure into the test items and arrive at structure from the responses.

As I discuss the construction of this dilemma and the principles and rules governing the analysis of responses in order to arrive at stage structure, keep before you Tables 2, 3, and 4. Table 2 represents a page from our manual for stage-scoring responses to the "mercy-killing" dilemma.

First a word about the alternate forms. For us, constructing a test with alternate forms for the assessment of developmental structure required a prior mapping out of the domain of content as well as a logical delimitation of the domain of structure. This was necessary, if only to hold content themes constant in constructing the alternate forms. The classification of content themes which we try to embody in our items and expect to provoke in the responses is derived from moral philosophy and the sociology of morals, in which disciplines attempts have been made to arrive at universal moral norms and issues. These themes, which we refer to as *elements* and *norms,* are listed in Table 3. In designing our test, we, the constructors, had to make a thematic analysis of content as well as consider issues of structure. The procedure in our manual requires that the test scorer be able to do the same.

I now turn to the process of scoring responses to the "mercy-killing" dilemma. Here you should keep before you Table 2.

The aim of the scorer is to arrive at stage structure, to discern the structure underlying responses. Before scorers can do this, they must perform successive classifications with regard to the content of the responses. The first involves a determination as to which of the two value issues in conflict the response falls under.

TABLE 2: Example of Moral Judgment Manual Item

Criterion Judgment #7

DILEMMA: IV
ISSUE: Law
NORM: Law
ELEMENT: Seeking reward (avoiding punishment), II.7
STAGE & SUBSTAGE: 2A

CRITERION JUDGMENT
[The doctor should not give the woman the drug] because he would risk losing his job or going to jail.
[NOTE: Do not match score this point if it is a response to the general question "Why is it important to obey the law?" unless the response refers to the doctor in this mercy-killing situation.]

STAGE STRUCTURE
Not killing the woman is justified because it involves a risk (rather than certainty) of punishment. Punishment is seen as something to be instrumentally avoided. The risk of punishment overrides the recognition of the pragmatic reasonableness from the woman's point of view of giving her the drug.

CRITICAL INDICATORS
One of the following must be used as the central justification for not killing the woman: (a) punishment as possible or probable, a risk to be weighed in the decision; OR (b) other disadvantageous consequences to the doctor (he might lost his job, etc.).

MATCH EXAMPLES
1. SHOULD THE DOCTOR GIVE HER THE DRUG THAT WOULD MAKE HER DIE? WHY?
   No, the doctor could be charged with killing her. He should give something to calm her. [WHY?] He would lose his career and go to prison. He should protect himself first and not kill her.
2. SHOULD THE DOCTOR GIVE HER THE DRUG THAT WOULD MAKE HER DIE? WHY?
   No. He would be blamed for killing her. She could take her own overdose. If he did, he could lose his license and be out of a job.

GUESS EXAMPLE
[NOTE: Guess scored only if no other scored material on the issue and weighted ½ match. Otherwise, material is a nonmatch.]
1. SHOULD THE DOCTOR DO WHAT SHE ASKS AND GIVE HER THE DRUG?
   No, I don't think so. I think it's asking too much of a doctor for one thing, that she should ask this even though she is in great pain. A doctor isn't supposed to do this. [WHY?] I believe it's in their code that you shouldn't give a drug to any person to help them die sooner or to put them to death right away. *If he were found out to have given her this drug, he'd probably be kicked out of his profession and he might not be able to get into something else.*
[NOTE: This refers to the likelihood that the doctor will lose his job as required by critical indicator (b), but the risk of undesirable consequences is not used as the central argument against mercy killing as the critical indicators specify.]

TABLE 3: The Elements and Norms for Classifying Content

THE ELEMENTS

I. MODAL ELEMENTS
1. Obeying (consulting) persons or deity. Should obey, get consent, (should consult, persuade).
2. Blaming (approving). Should be blamed for, disapproved (should be approved).
3. Retributing (exonerating). Should retribute against (should exonerate).
4. Having a right (having no right).
5. Having a duty (having no duty).

II. VALUE ELEMENTS

A. *Egoistic Consequences*
6. Good reputation (bad reputation).
7. Seeking reward (avoiding punishment).

B. *Utilitarian Consequences*
8. Good individual consequences (bad individual consequences).
9. Good group consequences (bad group consequences).

C. *Ideal or Harmony-Serving Consequences*
10. Upholding character.
11. Upholding self-respect.
12. Serving social ideal or harmony.
13. Serving human dignity and autonomy.

D. *Fairness*
14. Balancing perspectives or role taking.
15. Reciprocity or positive desert.
16. Maintaining equity and procedural fairness.
17. Maintaining social contract or freely agreeing.

THE NORMS

1. Life
   a) Preservation
   b) Quality/quantity

2. Property
3. Truth
4. Affiliation
(5. Erotic Love and Sex)
6. Authority
7. Law
8. Contract
(9. Civil Rights)
(10. Religion)
11. Conscience
12. Punishment

TABLE 4: **Example of Ego Development Manual Item**

ITEM 35: MY CONSCIENCE BOTHERS ME IF

DELTA

Characteristic Delta reactions displayed on this item are callousness ("I let it") and willful demanding ("always do what I want to do"). "I have to lie to someone who trusts me" displays also denial of responsibility for one's actions. "I can't have my own way" is illogical as an answer but clear as an expression of willfulness. Answers based on not succeeding or on being talked about indicate a lack of conscience almost as clearly as saying one does not have one. The one category here that names transgression of a rule refers to stealing; one may surmise that it is the concrete character of this transgression that impresses it on people earlier in development than lying or cheating.

1. —I STEAL ·
   If I take his money
   I take something that is not mine
2. —I DON'T HAVE A CONSCIENCE; MY CONSCIENCE NEVER BOTHERS ME
   none
   it doesn't
   I don't have any bothers
   always do what I want to
3. —I LET IT
   I realize it
4. —I AM BEING TALKED ABOUT, SUSPECTED
   my mother is suspicious of what I have been doing
   I feel that someone is watching me
5. —I HAPPEN, HAVE TO LIE, CHEAT, ETC. (I-3,1)
   I have to lie to someone who trusts me
   I happen to lie about something
   I am forced into a white lie
6. —I DON'T SUCCEED IN WHAT I WANT TO DO (I-3, 13; I-3/4, 14)
   I can't have my own way
   I'm inconsiderate & don't succeed in making a fool out of Jan
   do something stupid

UNCLASSIFIED
   I waste precious time taking tests like this

In the example in Table 2, the response falls under the category of upholding the law. This response in itself does not determine the stage structure of the response. Valuing law obedience may take place at any stage.

The second act of classification of content, therefore, is directed toward *determining the reasons* for valuing law obedience in this instance. These reasons take us closer to structure. As we have seen, Table 3 lists seventeen *elements of value*. These are derived from the efforts of moral philosophers to classify types of moral value. As you will note, the response in the example falls under Element 7, *avoiding punishment*. Now, one untutored in our system of scoring, or only superficially acquainted with it, might be led to conclude that the response is Stage 1 on the basis of this second act of content classification. But Stage 1 is not unequivocally indicated by a response reflecting the valuing of the element of punishment avoidance. The valuing of punishment avoidance may also emerge from a Stage 2 structure as it does in this case. An instrument is therefore needed to discriminate a Stage 2 from a Stage 1 structure where a punishment response is given. One such tool is a theoretical statement of Stage 2 structure pertaining to the issue of law and the element of punishment avoidance. This is presented in the paragraph called *Stage Structure* in the sample manual item of Table 2.

A second, and complementary, tool for arriving at stage structure is presented in the paragraph designated *Critical Indicators*. This category comprises those indicators reflecting whether a certain kind of set (here, a Stage 2 egoistically pragmatic set) is involved in thinking about punishment.

Consider now the examples of responses. The *match examples* pass the critical indicators. The *guess example* fails the critical indicators but seems to give some evidence of matching the stage structure of the manual item. A *fail example* would not only fail to embody the critical indicators but would suggest a different structure involved in valuing punishment avoidance than that characterizing Stage 2. For example, it might suggest valuing punishment avoidance in light of conventional-stage concerns for reputation in a societal context, rather than Stage 2 pragmatism.

Before contrasting this item from our manual with a parallel item from Loevinger's, let me review and elaborate some differences in our approaches. The concept of structure in Loevinger's scheme refers less to a form of thinking than to general stable and consistent personality content and function — the usage implied in psychoanalytic concepts of character structure. That is, structure in Loevinger's scheme is a hypothetical underlying entity of personality like the psychoanalytic ego. In contrast, the structure to which I refer is not potentially tangible. It is a construct to subsume a variety of different manifest responses. The responses of subjects to the dilemmas and their subsequent responses to clinical probing are taken to *reflect, exhibit,* or *manifest* the structure. They are the realizations of the "archetypal" structure in actuality, under special conditions. There may be disagreement by investigators concerning the correctness of the attribution of a certain structure, given certain responses (i.e., interrater reliability questions), but there can be no error in the sense of a mistake in inferring from a judgment to some state of affairs concurrent with, precedent to, or subsequent to the judgment. Thus, my procedure is not of the same order as that which one adopts in predicting from clouds to rain or smoke to fire or high white-cell count to appendicitis, or a response from an item on the MMPI to the conclusion of schizophrenia or hypochondriasis. Here one is dealing not with reflections, exhibitions, or manifestations but with indices or signs.

The sign approach fundamentally links signs to signs, and does not go beyond the manifest signs, in principle. My own approach does not go from sign to sign, but rather from expressions or "symbols" to what is postulated as a common theme or "structure." There is no way of discovering that structure or uncovering the structure as another sign. It is, in that sense, a construct rather than an inference, and is warranted only on the grounds of "intelligible" ordering of the manifest items. One might say that the hypothetical structure is the principle of organization of the responses. To treat it on the same level as the responses would be, in Ryle's sense, to commit a category mistake.

Because Loevinger sees her test items as signs which are

probabilistic indicators of an underlying personality organization, there is no need for her scoring categories to be structurally defined in the same sense that ours are. In fact, she does not make a clear distinction between structure and content in her stage definitions and scoring procedures. A look at one of her items illustrates this.

Table 4 presents an item from Loevinger's Sentence Completion Test. A comparison of the manual item from Loevinger with the one presented earlier from our own manual should illustrate both our differing conceptions of structure and the resulting differences in our approaches to test construction. To simplify comparison, I chose items holding content focus and stage structure constant. Both the Kohlberg and Loevinger items are moral in content, both are Stage 2 (Delta in Loevinger's scheme). If we impose on Loevinger's manual the distinctions between content and structure used in our own scoring system, the result is that some of her scoring categories do seem structural in our sense. That is, they are conceptually direct reflections of the organizational principles of the stage. Others are closer to what we would see as content. They may be logically consistent not only with the stage they represent but also other stages; in fact they are empirically most highly associated with the stage to which they are keyed.

Category 2 in the sample item comes fairly close to what we call structure but is still content associated with structure. The issue or content of value is our issue of conscience. Category 2 reflects a nonvaluing of this issue. We would call this an issue content value probabilistically associated with a Stage 2 structure, a devaluing of conscience which might probabilistically derive from an instrumental egoistic structure of valuing.

Category 1, "My conscience bothers me if I steal," is even farther than Category 2 from representing what we would call the structure represented by Loevinger's self-protective stage. The Loevinger manual notes that stealing is a more concrete content of moral valuing than lying or cheating. But in our terms, it is clearly content, a statement of what *is* wrong or right, not a direct expression of structure or of form of reasoning about *why* something is wrong or right.

Category 3 comes closer to representing the structure itself, as opposed to being a probable sign of the Delta stage. "My conscience bothers me if I let it" suggests that guilt and shame are affective states subject to ego control in light of an instrumental valuing of a purposive ego, rather than Stage I-2 impulses and feelings. It also suggests that guilt and shame have no legitimacy or value as representing social morality or social values, the hallmark of conventional thinking past the second stage. This kind of analysis is representative of what would be contained in the stage structure paragraph in our manual. It would not, however, appear in Loevinger's manual. Her manual does not include interpretive statements which explicate the structure of manual items and tie them to the overall structure of the stages they represent.

In terms of test methodology, the differences between Loevinger's epistemology and mine are expressed in differences in attitude to face validity, on the one hand, and to empirical item analysis on the other.

Our current test rejects both the sign approach and the selection and scoring of items through empirical item analysis. Each item must have face validity in representing the stage as defined by the theory. It cannot be placed at the stage simply because empirical item analysis indicates it has a probabilistic value as a sign of the stage.

Loevinger's assumptions in test construction are intermediate between the radical extremes of our Piagetian approach and the MMPI. She accepts the empirical sign approach of the MMPI, but only if it can be squared with some degree of logical or theoretical analysis, with some degree of face validity. She calls her approach one of saving circularity between theoretical logic and empirical item analysis.

In this context, "saving circularity" means a bootstrapping relation between the ego concept and empirical item analysis. As an example, the response "My conscience bothers me if I steal" has no clear face validity as reflecting a self-protective stage. If it had been initially placed at the conformist stage by clinical inference and theory, Loevinger would move it to her self-protective stage, on the basis of the item analysis which indicated that it is associated with clinical assignment of the total protocol to that stage. Loevinger calls it saving circularity rather than brute empiricism or empirically patching up the internal consistency or reliability of a test because it is a spiral process which modifies or improves the conception of each stage and not just the test's internal consistency or concurrent validity in the psychometric sense.

The evolution of my own theory and methods reflects a somewhat different kind of circularity or bootstrapping. I have already referred to the sequence anomalies which resulted from Kramer's original analysis of our longitudinal data (Kohlberg & Kramer, 1969). Several years of reflection led me to decide that the data called into question the construct validity of my measure rather than the truth of the Piagetian sequence hypothesis. More accurately, it led me to doubt some parts of the conceptual definitions of the stages underlying the rating guides which were our measures. Our stage definitions had confused content or surface structure with the deeper structure we meant to describe with our stages.

The reinterpretation led us to try to distinguish more clearly the structure from the content of the response in both stage definition and scoring. This led us first to a clinical rating of stage structure by a set of issue-rating guides, after classifying content by issue, as already described. Level of social perspective on the issue was the basis of rating. Stage 4, for example, was defined, not by valuing the issues of law and order, or the element of concern for the consequences to the group, but by a social system perspective.

The final step was to score a subsample of the cases clinically, with all the bias that implies, to see if we, not a skeptical audience, would have evidence confirming or disconfirming our sequence expectations. We found regular sequence in these ratings. We then constructed a standard interview with the same questions for all and developed a standardized scoring manual out of the responses to our longitudinal subsample in conjunction with our clinical rating guide. We then proceeded to blind score the remaining interviews for each of the 58 subjects in the longitudinal sample.

Our subjects were 10, 13, or 16 years old in 1956 and were interviewed every four years from then until 1977. Each interview included the presentation of nine hypothetical moral dilemmas —Interview Forms A, B, and C. The analysis of Form C has not yet been completed so I'll be reporting the results of Forms A and B.

Before going on to look at the results of the longitudinal study, let's look at the reliability of the scoring system. The test-retest figures are especially important because they give us the estimate of measurement error that is most relevant to our longitudinal analysis. Since we can't expect our measure to be error free, we need some estimate of measurement error against which to evaluate deviations from perfect sequentiality. Therefore, the analysis of longitudinal sequence involves a comparison of the frequency of sequence deviations or downward stage movement in the longitudinal data with the frequency of downward Time 1-Time 2 changes in our test-retest data. If sequence deviations exceed test-retest instability, we can't consider our data to support the invariant-sequence assumption.

Test-retest reliability figures are summarized in Table 5. As shown in that table, correlations between Time 1 and Time 2 for Forms A and B are both in the high .90's. Since the correlations could be very high without much absolute agreement between

TABLE 5: **Test-Retest Reliability of Standard-Form Scoring**

Correlation $T_1 - T_2$: Form A: .96 (Rater 1); .99 (Rater 2)
Form B: .97 (Rater 2)

Percent agreement within one-third stage: Form A 93%
Form B 94%
Forms A&B 100%

Percent agreement using pure-stage and mixed-stage scores [9 categories: 1, 1/2, 2, 2/3, 3, 3/4, 4, 4/5, 5]

Form A 70% (Rater 1), 77% (Rater 2) (N=43)
Form B 75% (Rater 2) (N=31)
Forms A&B 80% (Rater 2) (N=10)

Percent agreement using major/minor stage differentiations [13 categories: 1, 1(2), 2(1), 2, 2(3), 3(2), 3, 3(4), 4(3), 4, 4(5), 5(4), 5]

Form A 59% (Rater 1), 70% (Rater 2)
Form B 62% (Rater 2)
Forms A&B 70% (Rater 2)

scores at Time 1 and Time 2, we have also presented percent agreement figures. For almost all subjects, the scores on Times 1 and 2 were within one-third stage of each other. If we look at global scores based on a nine-point scale — the five stages and the four transition points between stages — we find between 70 and 80% complete agreement.

Overall, then, it appears that on two interviews conducted about a month apart almost all subjects receive scores within one-third stage of each other. About three quarters receive identical scores on the two interviews when a nine-point scale is used, and between one half and two thirds receive identical scores with the most finely differentiated thirteen-point scale.

Test-retest interviews described above were also used for assessing interrater reliability. The figures for interrater reliability (Table 6) look roughly comparable to the test-retest figures: Almost all interviews were scored within a third of a stage of each other by any two raters, and on about one half to two thirds of the interviews the two raters assigned identical scores even when using the thirteen-category system. The correlation between raters 1 and 2 was .98.

Alternate-form data are based on those test-retest subjects who received both Forms A and B and on the 233 longitudinal interviews which included both forms. A single rater scored independently both forms of the test-retest sample interviews. Percent agreement between Forms A and B for this sample was comparable to test-retest and interrater reliability: 100% of the interviews were given scores within one-third stage of each other for the two forms, 75% received identical scores for A and B using the nine-point scale, and 67% received identical scores for the two forms using the thirteen-point scale. The correlation between moral maturity scores for Forms A and B in this sample was .95.

The level of agreement across forms for the longitudinal data is not as high (see Table 7). This is to be expected since Form A was scored by rater 1 and Form B by rater 2. That is, the reliability figures confound form and rater differences.

A review of the correlational reliability data for the Standard Form indicates that the instrument is well within the limits of acceptable reliability. A comparison with related measures may

TABLE 6: **Interrater Reliability of Standard-Form Scoring**

Correlation, Raters 1 and 2, Form A test-retest interviews = .98

PERCENT AGREEMENT

rater pair	within 1/3 stage	complete agreement (9 categ.)	complete agreement (13 categ.)
FORM A			
1	100	88	53
2	100	88	63
3	100	75	63
4	88	88	63
5	88	88	63
FORM B			
6	100	78	78

TABLE 7: **Alternate-Form Reliability**

LONGITUDINAL SAMPLE (N=193)
    Correlation Form A - Form B = .84
        (Rater 1 for Form A, Rater 2 for Form B)
    85% agreement within 1/2 stage
        (other percent agreement figures not yet available)

TEST-RETEST SAMPLE
    Correlation Form A - Form B = .95
        (Rater 2 for both forms)
    Percent agreement (9 categories) = 75%
    Percent agreement (13 categories) = 67%
    Percent within 1/3 stage = 100%

be helpful here. Loevinger and Wessler (1970) report interrater reliability correlations for their Sentence Completion Test of ego development in the mid .80's, as compared to our correlations in the .90's. Jim Rest (1979) reports test-retest reliability in the .80's and internal consistency reliability in the .70's for the Defining Issues Test of moral development.

Considering percent agreement, the Standard Form again compares favorably with Loevinger's Sentence Completion Test. Interrater agreement on total protocol Sentence Completion score using a ten-point scale is reported to range from 50 to 80% (median 61%). This is substantially lower than the 75-88% that we obtain using our nine-point Standard Form Scale.

Turning to the longitudinal sample, let's look first at the sequence data. Table 8 presents global stage scores for Interview Forms A and B separately and for the two forms combined. The sequence reversals are noted with an X. In Form A these downward changes occurred in 7% of the adjacent time points (using our most differentiated thirteen-point scale of global interview scores). The reversals in Form B were 8%, and in Forms A and B combined were 7%. A comparison with downward stage change in test-retest data is presented in Table 9. You can see

TABLE 8: **Longitudinal Sequence**

Subject and Testing Time	Global Score Form A	Global Score Form B	Global Score Forms A&B Combined
1-1	*1	2	2(1)
1-2	1(2)	2	2(1)
1-3	2(3)	*2	2(3)
1-4	3(2)	3	3
1-6	4(3)	3(4)	4(3)
2-1	2(1)	2(1)	2(1)
2-2	3	3	3
2-3	4(3)	3(4)	3/4
2-4	3X	2(3)X	3(2)X
2-5	5(4)	4(5)	5(4)
2-6	5(4)	5(4)	5(4)
3-1	2(1)	2	2
3-2	2(3)	2(3)	2(3)
3-3	4(3)	3	3(4)
3-4	4(3)	3(4)	3(4)
3-5	4(3)	4(3)	4(3)
3-6	4(3)	4	4
4-1	2(3)	2	2
4-2	3	2(3)	3(2)
4-3	3(4)	3(2)	3
4-4	3(4)	*3(2)	3(4)
4-5	3(4)	4(3)	3(4)
5-1	2	1(2)	2(1)
5-2	2(3)	2	2(3)
5-3	2(3)	2(1)X	2X
5-4	3X	2	3(2)
5-5	3(2)	2	2(3)X
6-1	—	2(1)	2(1)
6-2	—	*2/3	2/3
6-3	—	3	3
6-4	—	3	3
6-5	—	*2/3	2/3X

Construction Case (rows 2-1 through 2-6)

X — reversal   * — scores were all guesses

TABLE 8 (cont.)

Subject and Testing Time	Global Score Form A	Global Score Form B	Global Score Forms A&B Combined
8-1	2	2(1)	2(1)
8-2	2	1X	2(1)
8-4	3(4)	3	3
9-1	2(1)	2(1)	2(1)
9-2	2(3)	2(3)	2(3)
9-3	3(2)	3	3
9-4	3	3	3
9-5	3(4)	3(4)	3(4)
9-6	4	*4(3)	4
11-1	1(2)	2	2(1)
11-2	3(2)	*2	2(3)
12-1	2	1(2)	2(1)
12-2	3	2	3(2)
12-3	3(4)	3(4)	3(4)
12-4	3(4)	3	3(4)
13-1	2(1)	2	2
13-2	2	2	2
13-5	3	3	3
14-1	3(2)	2	2(3)
14-2	2(4)(3)X	3(2)	3(2)
14-4	4	4	4
14-5	—	4(5)	4(5)
15-1	2(3)	2(3)	2(3)
15-2	3(2)	3	3(2)
16-1	3(2)	2(3)	2(3)
16-2	3(4)	3	3
16-3	4(3)	4(3)	4(3)
16-4	4	4	4
16-6	4	4	4

Construction Case (spanning rows 9-1 through 9-6)

TABLE 8 (cont.)

Subject and Testing Time	Global Score Form A	Global Score Form B	Global Score Forms A&B Combined
Construction Case 17-1	—	2	2
17-2	3(2)	2/3	3(2)
17-3	3(4)	3	3
17-4	3(4)	3	3(4)
17-5	4	4	4
17-6	4(5)	5(4)	4(5)
18-1	3	3	3
18-2	3(2)	3	3
18-4	3/4	3(4)	3(4)
18-5	3/4	*3/4	3/4
18-6	4	4	4
19-1	2	2(1)	2(1)
19-2	2/3	3(4)	3
19-4	3	3(4)	3(4)
19-5	3(4)	4(3)	4(3)
19-6	4(3)	4	4
21-1	2	*2(1)	2
21-2	3(2)	2	2(3)
21-3	3	2/3	3(2)
21-4	3(2)X	3	3
22-1	2	2(1)	2
22-2	2(1)X	2(3)	2(3)
22-3	4(3)	3(4)	4(3)
22-4	4(3)	4	4
22-5	4(3)	—	4(3)X
22-6	4	*4(5)	4
Construction Case 23-1	2	2(1)	2
23-2	2/3	3(4)	3(4)
23-3	3/4	4(3)	4(3)
23-4	4(3)	4(5)	4
23-5	4(5)	5	5(4)
23-6	5(4)	—	5(4)

TABLE 8 (cont.)

Subject and Testing Time	Global Score Form A	Global Score Form B	Global Score Forms A&B Combined
24-1	3	1(2)	2(1)
24-2	3	3(2)	3(2)
24-3	3(4)	3	3
24-4	3(4)	3(4)	3(4)
25-1	3(2)	2(1)	2(3)
25-2	3(4)	3	3
25-5	4(3)	4(3)	4(3)
25-6	4(3)	4	4
26-1	2	2	2
26-2	3	*3(2)	3
26-4	3	3	3
26-5	3	*3(4)	3
26-6	3(4)	3(4)	3(4)
27-1	2(3)	1(3)	3(2)
27-2	3(4)	3	3
27-4	4(3)	3	3(4)
27-5	3(4)X	3(4)	3(4)
29-1	2(3)	2(3)	2(3)
29-2	3	3	3
29-4	4(3)	3	3(4)
29-5	4	4(3)	4(3)
31-1	1(2)(3)	2	2(1)
31-2	3	2(3)	3(2)
31-5	3(4)	3(4)	3(4)
32-1	2(1)	2	2
32-2	2(3)	2	2
32-5	3	4(3)	3(4)
32-6	4(3)	4(3)	4(3)
36-1	2(3)	2(1)	2
36-2	2(1)(3)X	2	2
36-5	3(4)	3	3(4)
36-6	4(3)	3(4)	4(3)

TABLE 8 (cont.)

Subject and Testing Time	Global Score Form A	Global Score Form B	Global Score Forms A&B Combined
37-1	3	3(2)	3
37-2	3(4)	3(4)	3(4)
37-3	*4(3)	3(4)	3(4)
37-4	4	*4(5)	4
37-5	4(5)	5(4)	5(4)
37-6	—	5(4)	5(4)
38-1	2(3)	2	2
38-2	3(4)	3(4)	3(4)
38-5	3/4	4	4(3)
38-6	3/4	3(4)X	3(4)X
39-1	2(3)	2(3)	2(3)
39-2	3(4)	3	3(4)
39-3	3(4)	3	3X
39-4	4	4(3)	4
41-1	2/3	2	2
41-2	3(2)	3(2)	3(2)
41-3	3	3	3
41-4	3	3	3
41-5	3	3	3
41-6	4(3)	—	4(3)
Construction Case 42-1	3(2)	3(2)	3(2)
42-2	3	3	3
42-4	4(5)	4	4(5)
42-5	5(4)	4(5)	4(5)
42-6	5(4)	5(4)	5(4)
43-1	*3	3(2)(1)	3
43-2	3(4)	3/4	3(4)
43-3	4(3)	3/4	4(3)
43-4	4(3)	4(3)	4(3)
44-2	2(4)	3	3
44-3	4(5)	4(3)	4
44-4	4X	4	4
44-6	4(5)	4(5)	4(5)

TABLE 8 (cont.)

Subject and Testing Time	Global Score Form A	Global Score Form B	Global Score Forms A&B Combined
45-1	3(2)	2	2(3)
45-2	3	3(2)	3
45-4	4	4(3)	4(3)
45-5	4	4	4
45-6	4	4	4
47-1	2(3)	3(4)	3(2)
47-2	3(2)	3/4	3(4)
47-3	3	—	3X
47-4	3	3(4)	3(4)
47-5	3(4)	3(4)	3(4)
47-6	4(3)	2(4)X	4
48-1	2(3)	—	2(3)
48-2	3(4)	3(2)	3
48-4	4(3)	3	3(4)
48-5	4(3)	4(3)	4(3)
48-6	4(3)	4	4
49-1	3(4)	3	3
49-4	4(3)	4(3)	4(3)
49-5	3(4)X	3X	3(4)X
49-6	3(4)	4(3)	3(4)
50-1	3	3(2)	3
50-4	3(4)	3	3
50-5	4(3)	4	4
50-6	4(3)	4	4
51-1	2	2	2
51-4	3(4)	3(4)	3(4)
51-5	3/4	4	4(3)
51-6	3(4)	3(4)X	3(4)X
53-1	3	*3(1)(2)	3
53-2	3(4)	*3(2)(4)	3(4)
53-4	3X	3(4)	3(4)

TABLE 8 (cont.)

Subject and Testing Time	Global Score Form A	Global Score Form B	Global Score Forms A&B Combined
54-1	2(3)	2(3)	2(3)
54-5	3	3/4	3(4)
56-1	2	—	2
56-4	3	—	3
56-6	4(3)	—	4(3)
59-1	2(3)	1(2)	2(1)(3)
59-2	3	2/3	3(2)
59-4	3	3	3
59-5	3(4)	3(2)X	3
62-1	2(3)	3	3(2)
62-2	3(4)	4	4(3)
62-4	3X	*3X	3X
62-6	4(3)	4	4
64-1	3	3(2)	3
64-4	3	3(4)	3(4)
64-5	3(4)	4(3)	4(3)
Construction Case 65-1	3	3	3
65-2	4	*2X	4
65-4	4(3)X	4(3)	4(3)X
65-5	4(3)	4(3)	4(3)
65-6	4(3)	4	4
Construction Case 67-1	3	2(3)	3(2)
67-2	3	3	3
67-4	4(3)	3(4)	4(3)
67-5	4(5)	3(4)	4
67-6	5(4)	4(3)	4(5)
68-1	3	3	3
68-2	3(4)	3	3(4)
68-4	4(3)	3(4)	3(4)
68-5	4	*3(4)	4(3)
68-6	4	3X	4(3)

TABLE 8 (cont.)

Subject and Testing Time	Global Score Form A	Global Score Form B	Global Score Forms A&B Combined
70-1	2(3)	3(2)	3(2)
70-2	3(4)	3(4)	3(4)
70-4	3(4)	4(3)	4(3)
70-5	4	3(4)X	4(3)
70-6	3(4)X	4	4(3)
71-1	3	3	3
71-2	3(4)	3	3
71-4	4(3)	3(4)	3(4)
71-5	4(3)	3X	3(4)
81-1	3	2(1)	3(2)
81-2	3	3(2)	3(2)
81-5	4(3)	3(4)	3(4)
91-3	3	4(3)	3(4)
91-4	3(2)X	3X	3X
91-5	3(4)	3	3
91-6	4	4	4
92-3	3(2)	3	3(2)
92-4	3(4)	3(4)	3(4)
92-5	3X	*3(4)	3(4)
93-3	4(3)	3	3(4)
93-4	3(4)X	3	3(4)
93-5	3(4)	3(4)	3(4)
93-6	4(3)	4	4
95-3	3	3(2)	3
95-4	4(3)	—	4(3)
95-5	3(4)X	3	3X
95-6	—	3	3
96-3	4(3)	3	3(4)
96-4	3X	3	3X
96-5	4(3)	3(4)	3(4)
96-6	3(4)X	3X	3X

TABLE 9: Comparison of Downward Stage Change in Longitudinal* and Test-Retest Data

PURE- AND MIXED-STAGE SCORES

	Form A (Rater 1)	Form B (Rater 2)	Forms A&B combined
Longit. $T_n \to T_{n+1}$	2% (3/177)	4% (6/160)	1% (2/171)
Test-Retest $T_1 \to T_2$	19%	23%	10%

MAJOR/MINOR AND PURE-STAGE SCORES

	Form A	Form B	Forms A&B
Longit. $T_n \to T_{n+1}$	7%	8%	7%
Test-Retest $T_1 \to T_2$	19%	33%	20%

*Only the longitudinal interviews which were scored blind are included in this analysis.

that in every case the test-retest reversals are well over twice as great as the longitudinal reversals, so it seems reasonable to attribute the violations of longitudinal sequence to measurement error.

The concept of invariant stage sequence also implies that no stage will be omitted as development proceeds. In fact, if you look carefully at Table 8 you'll see that in no case on either form did a subject reach a stage in the sequence without having gone through each preceding stage. For the most part, changes across the four-year intervals were less than a full stage. According to the cognitive-developmental theory, the logic of each stage forms "a structured whole." In line with this assumption, one would expect to find a high degree of internal consistency in stage scores assigned. The data support this assumption as clearly as they do that of invariant sequence.

One indication of degree of internal consistency in moral judgment is provided by profiles for each subject of proportion of reasoning scored at each of the five stages. Our analysis of these profiles showed that most subjects received the great majority of their scores at either a single stage or at two adjacent stages. The mean percentage of reasoning at the individual's modal stage was 68% for Form A and 72% for Form B. Percentage of reasoning at the subject's most heavily used stages was 98% for Form A and 97% for Form B. (Remember that there are three dilemmas per form and that each dilemma was scored without knowledge of responses to the other dilemmas, so these figures cannot be an artifact of scorer bias.) The high correlations between alternate forms reported in the section on reliability provide further support for the consistency of a subject's stage of reasoning across differing content.

There remains a problem in interpreting these seemingly clear-cut results, however. It results from the circularity in the way the numbers were generated — a circularity that explains the differences between the results of Kramer's analysis (Kohlberg & Kramer, 1969) and the current one. From one extreme point of view, the data represent a desperate effort to save a theoretical hypothesis after it was disconfirmed by the Kramer data. From a second extreme point of view, they simply represent progress in an inductive description of stages.

To me, the most plausible point of view is neither inductive, nor hypothetico-deductive theory testing, but the point of view of what Loevinger calls "saving circularity" in the definition and measurement of a construct. Loevinger revised her stage definitions in light of empirical item analyses designed to increase the reliability and validity of her test. I did the circular revision not so much with the criterion of item consistency or reliability but with the criterion of sequence, our basic criterion of construct validity. From this point of view, the results in Table 8 define the construct validity of our test. I shall quote a statement about the appropriate criterion of construct validity of our moral stage measure which I made in my 1976 chapter in the Lickona volume:

> Construct validity means the fit of the data obtained by means of the test of primary components of its theoretical definition. The primary theoretical definition of structural moral development is that of an organization passing through invariant sequential stages (Kohlberg, 1976, p. 46).

In other words, data on longitudinal sequence tell us less about truth of theory than about the construct validity of a test based on the theory. It is less a synthetic or explanatory statement about nature than it is an analytic statement about structural stages. It says: Before you try to explain data of change and development with a cognitive-developmental theory, make sure your data can be observed with a measure you have made up to fit the sequence rule.

The same thing is true for assessments of reliability of stage tests. From the point of view of stage theories like Piaget's or mine, test reliability and test construct validity are one and the same thing. In the case of structural stage, construct validity demands high test-retest and alternate-form reliability. A stage is a structural whole; the individual should be consistent over various stimuli and occasions for testing structure. I don't have the time to expand, but our reliability data in Tables 5-7 fit this demand rather well.

I have already noted that there is a certain circularity involved in assumptions about truth of a theory and validity of a test. Only a bootstrapping spiral can make this a saving circularity. Loevinger's saving circularity is at the heart of scientific method in the epistemologies of pragmatism of Charles Sanders Peirce and John Dewey. It is the heart of the method which is neither induction nor deduction, but what Peirce called abduction. He compared scientific theory to a leaky boat you patch in one place and then stand on in another place while you patch or revise elsewhere. Sometimes the patching doesn't work and the boat sinks. But not, as Kuhn (1970) points out, until another boat comes along which the scientist can move to. I'd be happy to stop patching up Piagetian assumptions if I could see another boat on the horizon which handled my problems and data better than the stage concept. Until the critics point to that boat, I'm stuck with doing research with my test, one of a number of ways of doing useful research in moral development. Until that boat comes along, I might express the wish that psychologists interested in morality might get off stage bandwagons or antistage bandwagons and get on with the hard work of studying the enduring problems of moral development with the tools available. Our test is one.

Let me conclude that saving circularity doesn't always save all cherished assumptions. Sometimes one has to at least temporarily abandon a leaky stage boat without higher stage rescue. Our tables contain no Stage 6 scores. As far as we can ascertain all our Stage 6 persons must have been killed in the '60's like Martin Luther King. Stage 6 remains as a theoretical postulate but not an operational empirical entity.

Our discussion of the construct validity of the test has been restricted to its internal characteristics, structural wholeness and invariant sequence. There is a recurring demand to know about the validity of the test as a predictor to external criteria, particularly moral action or behavior. We have stated at the beginning of our talk that our test was a measure of judgmental competence necessary but not sufficient for real-life moral decision making and judgment. The study of real-life moral decision making we take up in the evening lecture.

TWO

Exploring the Moral Atmosphere of Institutions: A Bridge between Moral Judgment and Moral Action

In the previous lecture I reviewed our efforts to develop a test of moral stage. This test, which relies entirely on hypothetical dilemmas, is a test of moral *reasoning*. But the domain of morality encompasses more than just moral reasoning. The student of morality is concerned not only with moral *reasoning* but also with moral *action* — the process by which people arrive at moral decisions and take action on the basis of those decisions. By itself our test of moral stage is not a test of moral action. It asks the subject what any person morally *ought* to do in a particular hypothetical situation but not what that subject himself actually *would* do or *did* do in a particular *actual* situation. Thus we might say that our test of moral stage measures moral *competence* rather than *performance*. Our test is standardized in the sense that it relies on a fixed set of hypothetical dilemmas potentially meaningful to all persons rather than actual dilemmas faced by particular persons. For these reasons the test is the method of choice for testing general propositions of cognitive-developmental theory and propositions about the general process by which the structures of moral reasoning develop, and for evaluating educational change based on dilemma discussion. For the study of moral action, however, our test of moral stage is obviously not the method of choice. Consequently, my colleagues and I have tried to develop methods of studying moral action that go beyond the analysis of responses to hypothetical dilemmas.

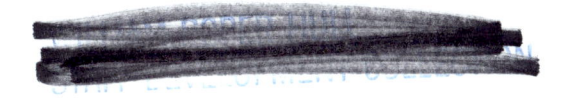

Before describing some of those methods, let me try to clarify what I mean by "moral action." Most studies in this area have relied on measures of moral action that define such action in behavioral terms, that is, in terms of the subject's conduct alone without regard for what that conduct means to the subject. For example, in the typical experiment designed to elicit "cheating," the investigator presents subjects with a situation in which correct responses cannot be given without cheating and then uses frequency of correct responses as a measure of "moral action." But without inquiring into the motives and judgments that underlie a subject's decision to "cheat" in this kind of experiment, one is in no position to determine whether the subject's conduct belongs to the moral domain or not. Without making such an inquiry, we have no way of knowing whether the subject defines the experimental situation as one in which moral issues are raised, or whether he has reached his decision on moral grounds. Action is not *moral* action unless it is generated by moral reasoning and motives. Thus we cannot study moral action merely by observing behavior defined a priori as "moral." Rather, we must inquire into the processes of moral judgment and decision making that necessarily underlie moral action, as well as the action itself.

Moral action, as I have defined it, must be studied in naturalistic settings. If we are to understand moral action as it actually occurs, we must take a direct approach: We must study the process by which people resolve the dilemmas that they actually face in their lives. And our measures of moral action must be clinical rather than standardized. Rather than scoring subjects on the basis of a protocol consisting of a fixed set of items, we must delve into their actual moral experience by means of an open-ended interview. Whereas moral judgment interviews are designed to tap *hypothetical* reasoning, moral action interviews are designed to elicit *practical* reasoning, that is, reasoning about what the subject actually *would* or *did* do in a particular dilemma. Practical reasoning differs from hypothetical reasoning in that it has a *descriptive* as well as a *prescriptive* component. In hypothetical reasoning the facts of the dilemma are taken as given.

Practical reasoning, on the other hand, is reasoning about what the facts of the situation are as well as what one's obligation in that situation is. Thus moral action interviews, unlike moral judgment interviews, attempt to tap the subject's factual perceptions — his perceptions of his own actual conduct as well as other factual aspects of the situation. Examples of this general approach to the study of moral action may be found in the work of several of my colleagues. Carol Gilligan has undertaken a study of women's reasoning, decision making, and action when faced with the issue of whether to have an abortion. Bob Selman and Dan Jaquette (1977) are studying students' practical reasoning produced spontaneously in activity groups. Here at Clark, Bill Damon's (1977) work also bridges the gap between moral reasoning and action by means of simultaneous interviewing and observation.

My own studies have assumed that intensive naturalistic examination of the process of moral decision making and action in real life should be guided not only by general *theoretical* interests, but by practical and educational interests as well. My experience working with educators led me to rethink the relationship of theory to practice in ways which have implications for both moral education and the naturalistic study of moral action. When I started working in educational settings, I attempted to deduce practices the teacher should use from my research-based psychological theory as embodied in the Blatt dilemma-discussion method. I related theory to practice in the same way as B.F. Skinner and other psychologist colleagues. I now view that way of relating theory to practice as "the psychologist's fallacy." The "psychologist's fallacy" is the assumption that the variables important for psychologists to research are the important variables for teachers to think about, or should be the foundation of valid thinking about educational practice. The relationship between psychology and education must be a two-way street, rather than starting with pure-theory concepts. It follows that the psychologist's naturalistic study of moral action can be of use to the practitioner in discerning those aspects of moral decision making which have specific relevance to his or her content area. For example, the abortion study of Gilligan, mentioned earlier, can be of great value to an abortion counselor. In the research we discuss today we focus on a natural concept of concern to teachers and students, the concept of school community.

One of the most important assumptions that we have made in studying this area is that individual moral action usually takes place in a social or group context and that that context usually has a profound influence on the moral decision making of individuals. Individual moral decisions in real life are almost always made in the context of group norms or group decision-making processes. Moreover, individual moral action is often a function of these norms or processes. For example, in the massacre at My Lai, individual American soldiers murdered noncombatant women and children. They did so not primarily because, as individuals, they judged that action to be morally right, nor because, as individuals, they were "sick" in some sense, but because they participated in what was essentially a group action taken on the basis of group norms. The moral choice made by each individual soldier who pulled the trigger was embedded in the larger institutional context of the army and its decision-making procedures. Their decisions were dependent in large part upon a collectively shared definition of the situation and of what should be done about it. In short, the My Lai massacre was more a function of the group "moral atmosphere" that prevailed in that place at that time than of the stage of moral development of the individuals present. The realization of the important role that moral atmosphere or group norms play in individual moral action has led us to hypothesize that in many cases the best approach to moral education is one that attempts to reform the moral atmosphere in which individual decisions are made. This is the hypothesis that has guided our interventions and research in the schools and prisons.

In our school interventions, our educational interest focused upon improving the moral decisions of the group, of the classroom community as such, rather than focusing only upon individual moral change. We saw the task of changing group decisions as implying something more than changing the average stage of the individual members making decisions. It meant a concern for developing the shared norms and expectations of the school community. Our hypothesis was that such direct efforts to raise the collective moral level would stimulate individual moral judgment advance. In addition, we thought that raising the group level would have an effect on the actual moral conduct of the students. Our assumptions about changing individual values through working with the group qua group derive mainly from two theories — those of Kurt Lewin (1947) and Emile Durkheim (1961). Lewin stressed that individual value change occurred where individuals were committed to a group that decided to change its values. The conditions for value change were strong group cohesion and strong shared attraction to the group. According to Lewin, a democratically led group produces strong group cohesion and more cooperative attitudes than does an authoritarian group, a claim documented in the study of Lippitt and White (1943).

Whereas Lewin claimed that group cohesion could contribute to individual value change, he did not provide a conceptualization of the moral dimension of the group and its effects on values and attitudes. For a development of the moral dimension, we have turned to the theory of Durkheim. Durkheim proposes that real-life moral judgments and acts spring directly from the experience of group life. He holds that the spirit of discipline and the moral rules and norms that bind and obligate us do so because they are socially shared and embody the authority of the group that holds them. In a complementary way, the more altruistic impulses to caring and sharing also move us when they are felt to be shared, when they are based on a sense of shared affection for the collectivity. Accordingly, the development of morality depends for Durkheim upon the child's membership in a group whose authority he respects and with which he feels strong solidarity.

The school group is, for Durkheim, a necessary one for moral development because it is intermediary between the family and the larger society. He says:

> That which is essential to the spirit of discipline, respect for the rules and duty, can scarcely develop in the family which is not subject to general impersonal regulation. That which is essential to commitment toward collective ends, a feeling and affection for the collectivity, can also not arise in the family where solidarity is based on blood ties and intimate relations. To promote the inclination to collective life one must get hold of the child when he leaves the family and enters the school (Durkheim, 1961, p. 148).

Durkheim tells us two characteristics that a classroom must have if it is to build morality. The first is formal rules that embody group authority. The second is strong group cohesion or a sense of community. These two dimensions of a good moral atmosphere Durkheim sees as dependent upon the teacher's wise and moral use of authority. As an example, Durkheim says the teacher should build community through the use of collective punishment and reward: "Collective sanctions play a very important part in the life of the classroom. The most powerful means to instill in children the feeling of solidarity are to feel that the value of each is a function of the worth of all" (Durkheim, 1961, p. 239).

Durkheim's approach is authoritarian in the sense that he does not allow for the possibility that a peer group might develop a good moral atmosphere in the absence of authority. In his view, for example, an unregulated delinquent gang would be assumed to have little sense of discipline or solidarity. The moral nature of the group partly depends on the moral authority of the teacher, which represents the authority of the group.

The Lewin-Durkheim approach is, of course, not directed toward influencing the *stage* or *structure* of group norms and values but toward influencing their *content*. Implicit in Durkheim's thinking, however, is a structural stage concept. His definition of the elements of morality, of the spirit of discipline and duty, the spirit of altruism, aspiration and liberty, presupposes Stage 4 moral judgment.

The Durkheim theory is not only a theory of moral learning, but also defines an ideology or social philosophy. This is the communitarian ideology, which says that the ideal human society is predicated upon the sharing of resources, values, goals, and interests. This communitarian ideology is often associated with democracy, ideals of equality, and the sharing of power as well as of resources and concerns.

The communitarian ideology is central to a left-wing Israeli kibbutz, whose moral education practices were studied by Joe Reimer (1977) and myself (Kohlberg, 1971). These practices center on the *kvutza*, an age group of twenty to thirty high school students whose group life is heavily influenced by the *madrich*. The *madrich*, also a teacher, has as his most important function that of group leader. Decisions about rules and moral conflicts are made by the group, with the *madrich* having little formal authority, but an informal authority that makes him more than first among equals.

The *madrich* we came to know best explicitly held the Durkheim theory. He held that the creation of group rules and obligations is important, not simply for their content, but also as a means of creating a moral attitude toward the group and of maintaining community solidarity. Reciprocally, he thought that the sense of community or group cohesion was necessary for the development of moral attitudes toward rules and their enforcement. The *madrich* told us:

> Our methods of education depend upon the group. For 24 hours the adolescent lives with other members of the group. He has to be affected by the group if we are to succeed. For instance, do you know about the system of studying here? The system is no examination, no punishment. Because in itself punishment by the adult has no meaning. The most we can do is to throw a ward out, and that only really happens when he doesn't want to belong to the group anymore. We can come to a person and tell him, "Go and study, go and learn." He says, "If I don't study, what are you going to do to me?" And I say, "Nothing." So I have to use the group. I can go to the group and say, "Look, this one, and one or two others, they don't study, they don't participate in class, they are slowing down the progression of the whole group in learning." And so he can say to me, "I don't care," but the group can put the pressure on him. If he cares for the group and has a good relationship with the others, he might change his ways. If the group is strong, if it has solidarity, it works.

Not surprisingly, the collective form of moral education is extremely effective in stimulating the development of Stage 3 and Stage 4 morality. Half of the students in the particular kibbutz high school studied were disadvantaged city children placed on the kibbutz by a social agency. These children entered the kibbutz school primarily at the second stage on the hypothetical dilemmas. Ordinarily, the majority of such children would not be expected to progress beyond Stage 2. Yet all moved to the third or fourth stage in the high school period, as measured by standard hypothetical dilemmas. Moreover, student reasoning about real-life decisions also developed to conventional stages. These changes were reflected in interviews about real-life decisions in the school, and were confirmed by other forms of observation.

I have noted that the interviews of the students were naturalistic and clinical and dealt with real-life moral dilemmas. To understand these interviews, however, we must note that they were about not only the individual's moral decision making but also the moral atmosphere of his group. They make it clear that the student's decisions were not purely a function of his individual psychological stage, but were also a function of his perception of the collective norms of the group, and his reaction to those views in terms of his role as group member.

As an example, consider this statement by Ehud on the subject of stealing:

> If someone in the group steals, they will call a meeting. If it's a one-time occurrence, they'll take it back and ask him not to do it again. Everyone in the group knows it's not worth breaking the social agreement. In the city they have laws, but on the kibbutz, in place of laws there are social agreements. Social agreements are found both in the city and the kibbutz, like honor your parents. But let's say that one day on kibbutz a student is angry and doesn't feel like studying. He knows that it is wrong, but they won't do anything to him. Maybe yell at him but they won't punish him. Everyone has to live with his own conscience.

Ehud tells us about the collective norms of the group, both those concerned with stealing and those concerned with studying. The norms are not generated simply by his own individual structures of moral judgment, nor are they simply perceptions of society's laws. Prior to entering the kibbutz, Ehud presumably did not regard the norms about studying as moral norms. Yet these norms became moral for him; they became a source of moral disapproval on the part of other group members and the basis for the creation of conscience in the individual.

Our school decision-making interview is thus a moral atmosphere interview; it tells us about the collective norms and expectations of the group. The interview from which I have quoted clearly supports the Durkheimian theory of moral education as it applied in certain kibbutz educational practices, in that it demonstrates the moral force of the group as discussed by Durkheim. It indicates that the student's moral action is governed by "the spirit of discipline," by respect for rules that embody the authority of the group to which he belongs. It is also governed by the "spirit of altruism," by the norms of positive group solidarity or community that Durkheim stresses as the second moral dimension of the group.

We have used the kibbutz to present Durkheim's theory of collective moral education and to show how interviews about concrete moral decisions become moral atmosphere interviews. We now shift to our own modified use of a Durkheimian theory of collective moral education in an American alternative school. This alternative school, called the Cluster School, is a democratically governed institution that I helped to establish in 1974. It is composed of approximately sixty-five students and six staff members and is housed in a large urban high school. Once a week everyone in the school meets to hold discussions and make decisions through majority vote about issues of governance. The staff attempts to prepare the students for the community meeting by highlighting the moral dimensions of the issues that arise, so that these will be recognized and dealt with. The hope is that students will carefully make, uphold, and enforce decisions which are fair to individuals and which lead to the building of a community.

It is in this context that Joe Reimer, Clark Power, Ann Higgins, Marvin Berkowitz, Anat Abrahami, and I have developed a structural analysis of moral atmosphere (Power, 1979). Our analysis relies on three forms of data — transcripts of the weekly community meetings, interviews with students about the nature of the school and their own role in it, and interviews about recurring school-relevant moral dilemmas.

The theory employed by the school was not solely the collectivistic or communitarian theory of Durkheim. Equally central were the democratic and interactional theories of John Dewey and Piaget.

Dewey (1966) insisted that morality develops through role taking occurring in, or reciprocal interaction among, individuals, implying a need for school democracy or decision making on the basis of equality and open interchange. Piaget, in *The Moral Judgment of the Child* (1932), picks up Dewey's theory and contrasts an early morality of heteronomous respect with a later morality of contract and mutual respect. From this point of view a good moral atmosphere is a democratic and cooperative one.

In the remaining time, I shall discuss the development of the moral atmosphere of the Cluster School in its first two years of existence. The data are based primarily on two sources. The first is the transcripts of the weekly community meetings of the school. The second is the interviews given every year to the students themselves.

Our major hypothesis was that in some sense the group or collective norms developed in stages over time in a way distinguishable from the change in individual social or moral judgments also going on. We shall discuss this development first in terms of statements in the community meetings.

Statements in community meetings do not only express individual moral judgments. They also appeal to collective norms, to norms believed to be shared with other members of the group. As an example, in a community meeting John says: "All the people in this community right now are all saying in some way or other that they care about one another." John is asserting that there is a shared or collective norm that each member care about the others. To the extent that other speakers seem to agree or to make similar statements, we can assert that there is a collective norm of caring, and trace its evolution in terms of the stage structure used by the students to interpret its meaning and to justify it.

We shall illustrate the development of collective norms in Cluster School in its first two years by considering the statements made by students and staff in two meetings, each dealing with episodes of stealing. The two meetings were a little less than a year apart. In the first meeting, there was evidence of little in the way of collective norms of trust maintenance, caring, or other values relevant to stealing. Student judgments were largely individualistic, and primarily at the second stage. In this meeting, recurrent episodes of stealing led students to suggest making a rule requiring restitution if someone was detected stealing. The reasoning was pragmatic: Individuals would want their property back. Violation of trust was not judged unethical. Students said that if you were stolen from it was largely your fault for being careless, and that one could never know whom to trust. Staff members persisted in asking about the wrongness of stealing and the norms it violated: for example, "Don't people think it's wrong and a violation of the community?" or "Ripping off is not an individual business; it's a community business. People have to have some level of trust or it's no community." Student responses were on the order of, "The fact is it happened. To worry about why it happened isn't worth it" or, "You teachers are always on our backs. We've made a rule, what more can you want?"

In the second meeting students begin making reference to collective norms of trust and caring. This meeting was precipitated by a stealing incident in which nine dollars was stolen from someone's purse and no one would admit to the theft. One group of students came to the meeting with a proposal that each member of the school should chip in fifteen cents to make up for the nine dollars stolen from the girl's purse. Phyllis, a girl from this group, offered the following rationale for reimbursing the stolen money. "It's everyone's fault that she don't have no money. It was stolen because people just don't care about the community." They think "they are all individuals and don't have to be included in the community." "Everybody should care that she got her money stolen," and therefore "we decided to give her money back to her." Staff members and students both pointed out that the community should put pressure on the guilty party to return the money. Thus they adopted a compromise: "If the money is not returned anonymously by a certain date, everyone will be assessed fifteen cents." The combined proposal was voted in and in fact proved effective. There were no thefts in the school in the two years following the meeting. As one girl put it, "If you want to rip off, rip off in your own time, not in school, not in Cluster School."

In comparing these two meetings we do not think that development in individual moral judgment between year one and year two can alone account for the change in stealing behavior. A review of the transcripts will show some individual reasoning at Stage 2 and Stage 3 in each meeting. What has changed dramatically is the social context in which judgments are being made. We maintain that in its second year, Cluster School progressed toward becoming a third-stage just community. Phyllis' statements marked the change. They revealed a Stage 3 structure not only of Phyllis' individual moral judgment but of the moral atmosphere of the Cluster community. Phyllis did not simply speak for herself as an individual with personal opinions. In her view students were obligated qua members of the community to live up to these expectations. Thus caring and trust were no longer perceived as simply being the staff's bag of virtues but were seen as values that the community as a whole was beginning to share. We refer to these shared values as "collective normative values," distinguishing them from values expressed in individual moral judgments. Phyllis' statement presumed the existence of a norm — a generalized expectation that no one would steal. That norm was linked to the normative values of caring and trust, so that there was a generalized expectation that not only would individual members not steal the property of others, but that they would also actively care for the property of others and see that no one else stole it.

What gave force to these normative values was their being perceived as necessary for creating a community in the school. The staff in the first year suggested that the issue of stealing be viewed as "a violation of the community," but only one student responded to that. By the second year, students were concerned with whether the school was "really a community." This concern presupposed the recognition that "this school is supposed to be a community." We believe this recognition was crucial for the resolution of the stealing problem.

We have given an illustration of stage movement in statements which reflect growth in collective norms. We turn now to moral atmosphere interview data to illustrate stage growth. We shall focus upon the development of students' ideals and conceptions of school community, as they move from the second to the fourth stage. At first we will look at these as reflecting growth in the individual cognitive structures of the student interviewed. Then we shall attempt to show that this growth represents a growth in shared ideals and expectations of the students, not simply the growth of each student's changing ideals and conceptions in isolation.

Our first subject, Jane, illustrates movement from a second-stage to a third-stage ideal of community. This growth illustrates the notion of the term community, since the second-stage conception is not really a conception of community at all. In our previous discussion of community we equated it with sharing and with the spirit of cohesion. In the sociological literature the term *Gemeinschaft*, or community, is typically contrasted with the term *Gesellschaft*, society or association. Community implies an internally valued set of relations, and sharings. Association suggests that social relations or groups are valued instrumentally in aiding the individual's purposes or guaranteeing his rights. In this sense, an ideal of community as distinct from association seems to be only meaningful at our third stage and later. Table 10 suggests this in its comparison of the second and third stage of community.

TABLE 10: Stages of Collective Normative Values and the Sense of Community

COLLECTIVE NORMATIVE VALUES	SENSE OF COMMUNITY
STAGE 2	
There is not yet an explicit awareness of collective normative values. However, there are generalized expectations that individuals should recognize concrete individual rights and resolve conflicts through exchange. *Examples:* 1. Do not "rat" on another group member. Ratting or reporting another group member to authorities is disapproved of because it exposes the rule breaker to likely punishment. 2. Do not bother others. Live and let live. 3. Help others out when you want to.	There is no clear sense of community apart from exchanges among group members. Community denotes a collection of individuals who do favors for each other and rely on each other for protection. Community is valued insofar as it meets the concrete needs of its members. *Example:* The community is like a "bank." Members meet to exchange favors but you cannot take more than you give.
STAGE 3	
Collective normative values refer to relationships among group members. Membership in a group implies living up to shared expectations. Conflicts should be resolved by appeal to mutual collective normative values. *Examples:* 1. Members of a group should be able to trust each other with their possessions. 2. Members of a group should care about other members of the group.	The sense of community refers to a set of relationships and sharings among group members. The group is valued for the friendliness of its members. The value of the group is equated with the value of its collective normative expectations. *Examples:* 1. The community is a family in which members care for each other. 2. The community is honorable because it helps others.
STAGE 4	
Collective normative values stress the community as an entity distinct from its individual members. Members are obligated to act out of concern for the welfare and harmony of the group. *Examples:* 1. Individuals not only are responsible for themselves but share responsibility for the whole group. 2. Individuals should participate in the political organization of the group by making their opinions known and by being informed voters.	The school is explicitly valued as an entity distinct from the relationships among its members. Group commitments and ideals are valued. The community is perceived as an organic whole composed of interrelated systems that carry on the functioning of the group. *Example:* Stealing affects "the community more than the individual because that is what we are. We are not just a group of individuals."

Before giving a case illustration, we should note that concepts like community or democracy are not universal concepts like friendship or parenthood — concepts which exist in all children. All children have concepts of group; some communitarian ideal of a group presupposes exposure to a group with more communitarian ideals. Jane came into the school in its second year, when many students articulated ideals of community. But in the middle of her first year in Cluster School Jane does not have such a conception of community, even though such a conception was verbally taught in social studies. Asked, "Do you take the courses in communities?," she answers "Yes, on Fridays." "Did they talk about the difference between an association and a community?" She says, "Yes, in an association you go for a purpose, in a community we go on trips and we get together. We don't talk about one thing, we talk about a lot of things." For Jane the distinction between an association and a community is the difference between a work group and a play group. Insofar as the idea of community implies obligation or moral ideal, it is one of "going along with the gang." We asked, "In your street group, how do you decide things?" and she replied, "If kids want to go they go, if they don't they don't." We asked, "How about in Cluster?" and she said, "You should go. If you are going to belong to that school, why not go? Because that is what the school is made of — going on trips and talking. If they don't want to go they don't have to, but it is a community so they should go on trips and all stay together."

Jane, then, has one norm of community — physical cohesion. A second norm is "getting along with one another." She says, "We all get along with one another. Out there in the high school they beat each other up. Out in the high school some white kids threatened Kate because she voted to let black kids in. Here black and white get along real good."

One year later, Jane has moved from the second-stage conception of community to a third-stage conception. She sees most members of the school acting for a common goal, "making a good school." She says, "I think the school is a community on one basis, where we all get together and we are all striving for one thing. A really good school."

She now defines community in terms of all sharing in valuing the school or group intrinsically, making it a good school.

One year later, Jane moves to the beginning of a fourth-stage ideal of community. One aspect of this fourth-stage ideal is the beginning of the idea of a general will, of a group of people all thinking in terms of the community's welfare. She says, "The school is a community because everybody speaks out what he or she feels to come to a decision. And the decision is made by everybody, they are different people but it is still a whole in which everybody is participating."

At a third stage, Jane saw community as the prior goals and values shared by the individuals composing the group. Now she sees the community as an organic whole trying to unite individual voices into common decisions. The community is a gestalt different from the sum of its individual members and what they come into the group sharing.

Another aspect of Jane's beginning fourth-stage conception of community is that of generalized obligations of respect and caring for all other members, regardless of accidents of friendship and clique. She says, "In this school people should respect one another and listen even though they don't agree. They want to care and they do care because this is a community and that is what you must do in a community."

Jane echoes Durkheim, then, about the obligation to be altruistic to other individuals as arising from depending upon solidarity with the group as a whole. She says, "In a democratic community we can't have selfish people who just talk of themselves. There are a lot of people who loved the community and put a lot into it and it is hard to accept that somebody doesn't care."

One other subject, Eileen, may clarify the passage from Stage 3 to Stage 4 normative conceptions of community. Eileen entered the school in its first year. At that time, like Jane in her first year, she had no clear conception of community in the Stage 3 sense. In the second year of the school she clearly articulates a Stage 3 conception of community. She says, "People are supposed to be a community and not like outside. You should be able to leave something and not worry that it will be stolen. In the high school everyone wants to do his thing and get what *I* want — me. Here we're trying to think more of we."

In the third year of the school Eileen begins to articulate a fourth-stage conception of community. She tries to make decisions in terms of the general welfare or the general will. She says, "When I vote in the community meeting I think about what my vote will do as a whole to everyone in the community. Most of the rules don't bother me. But I think: If this passes, what people will be able to go by it and what people won't?"

Eileen also clearly articulates the distinction between an integrated Stage 4 community, and subgroups and cliques viewed more in Stage 3 terms. She says, "This school is supposed to be a community and everybody is supposed to be together, but I still find there are cliques, different backgrounds and neighborhoods. But I think for the environment we are in, it's probably about as much of a community as you are going to get."

We have illustrated the progression in normative ideals of community in relation to school perception of the students moving from Stage 2 to 3 and to the beginnings of fourth-stage thinking. We now need to clarify the sense in which the movement in defining community represents a movement in shared collective ideals and expectations. In the same period, these two students were also moving from Stage 2 to 3 to 4 on our standard dilemmas. This movement, however, is the movement of each as individuals, though it is movement partly responsive to a common school environment. We would argue, however, that the movement from Stage 2, community as common activities and getting along, to Stage 3 notions of being a "we" with common goals is not a movement of each student isolatedly restructuring his cognitive framework. The perception that we are a "we" is a collective movement. No single individual student could develop a sense of we without others developing in that direction. Students would not want identical Stage 3 responses to the Heinz dilemma; it would be "copying"; but in some sense they strive to achieve common definitions in what we assess in the moral atmosphere interview.

As collective development of a moral atmosphere is not inevitable, the students, once having developed a fourth-stage concept of community, will always keep this as a cognitive construction and as an ideal. The actual collective functioning and norms may, however, regress in stage, or the collective norms may lose their force.

What is the value of the kind of stage development we assess with our moral atmosphere interview? It is valuable insofar as the creation of a particular just community is valuable. Where individuals are life-long members of a community, advance in the stage of justice and community in a group is obviously worthwhile. Insofar as students in a kibbutz or the kibbutz as a collectivity moves or grows toward fourth- or fifth-stage shared norms of trust, concern, and collective responsibility, then life is moral, and people do treat each other morally.

What is the situation, however, where students have a community with fourth- or fifth-stage collective norms of justice and community, and then go out to a world where these norms are not shared? Hopefully what is retained is a higher stage of individual moral reasoning, a history of action in terms of these norms, and the ability to help make or move groups of which the person is a member to a higher stage. We don't know if that will be the case but that was John Dewey's vision for the schools —that schools would make citizens who were more just and democratic, and who would then make schools and the society more just in a progressive spiral. Whether Dewey's noble vision can become more real or not, I do not know. It is at least a worthwhile enough vision to justify the small research effort my colleagues and I have mounted on moral atmosphere.

We started with the problem of studying moral action but our discussion has been about words in community meetings and in interviews. But words in community meetings are group action; they establish rules and policies. When in the second year the group voted for collective restitution, they instituted a policy reported on subsequent occasions. When they collectively endorsed the need to maintain trust, incidents of stealing within the group vanished. Gross frequencies of actions violating norms or maintaining them for groups are easier to obtain than records of individual behavior and give gross support to what is said in community meetings. Things said in community meetings are real moral judgments — they represent a certain degree of commitment to the reasons and policies advocated. And changes in what is said in moral atmosphere interviews by our two students correspond to changes in their judgments and proposals in community meetings. When Jane entered the third stage she became an active advocate and maintainer of the norms, a good citizen.

One may, of course, question at a deeper level whether words in meetings making social policies represent the real reasons for the policies and actions in question. This is, of course, the legitimate question asked by Marxists and Freudians researching for interests and motives underneath shared ideologies.

To even ask such questions, however, assumes that we have some understanding of the more manifest structure of decision making and judgment. We think our stage-structural approach to social or moral atmosphere does at least carry us far in that step toward understanding moral action.

REFERENCES

Baldwin, J.M. *Social and ethical interpretations in mental development.* New York: Macmillan, 1897.

Blatt, M.M., & Kohlberg, L. The effects of classroom discussion upon children's level of moral judgment. *Journal of Moral Education,* 1975, *4,* 129-161.

Colby, A., Kohlberg, L., Gibbs, J., Candee, D., Speicher-Dubin, B., & Power, C. *Assessing moral judgment stages: A manual.* Cambridge, Mass.: Moral Education Research Foundation, 1978.

Damon, W. *The social world of the child.* San Francisco: Jossey-Bass, 1977.

Dewey, J. *Democracy and education.* New York: Free Press, 1966. (Originally published, 1916.)

Dewey, J., & Tufts, J.H. *Ethics.* (Rev. ed.). New York: Holt, 1932.

Durkheim, E. *Moral education: A study in the theory and application in the sociology of education.* New York: Free Press, 1961. (Originally published, 1925.)

Kohlberg, L. *The development of modes of moral thinking and choice in the years ten to sixteen.* Unpublished doctoral dissertation, University of Chicago, 1958.

Kohlberg, L. Stage and sequence, the cognitive-developmental approach to socialization. In D. Goslin (Ed.), *Handbook of socialization theory and research.* New York: Rand McNally, 1969.

Kohlberg, L. Cognitive-developmental theory and the practice of collective moral education. In M. Wolins & M. Gottesman (Eds.), *Group care, an Israeli approach: The education path of youth Aliyah.* New York: Gordon and Breach, 1971.

Kohlberg, L. Continuities in childhood and adult moral development revisited. In P.B. Baltes and K.W. Schaie (Eds.), *Life-span developmental psychology: Personality and socialization.* New York and London: Academic Press, 1973.

Kohlberg, L. Moral stages and moralization: The cognitive-developmental approach. In T. Lickona (Ed.), *Moral development and behavior: Theory, research, and social issues.* New York: Holt, Rinehart and Winston, 1976.

Kohlberg, L., & Kramer, R. Continuities and discontinuities in childhood and adult moral development. *Human Development,* 1969, *12,* 93-120.

Kuhn, T.S. *The structure of scientific revolutions.* (2nd ed.). Chicago, Ill.: University of Chicago Press, 1970.

Kurtines, W., & Grief, E. The development of moral thought: Review and evaluation of Kohlberg's approach. *Psychological Bulletin,* 1974, *81,* 453-470.

Lambert, H.V. *A comparison of Jane Loevinger's theory of ego development and Lawrence Kohlberg's theory of moral development.* Unpublished doctoral dissertation, University of Chicago, 1972.

Lewin, K. Group decision and social change. In T. Newcomb & E. Hartley (Eds.), *Readings in social psychology.* New York: Henry Holt, 1947.

Lippitt, R., & White, R.K. The social climate of children's groups. In R.G. Barker, J.S. Kounin, & H.F. Wright (Eds.), *Child behavior and development.* New York: McGraw-Hill, 1943.

Loevinger, J. The meaning and measurement of ego development. *American Psychologist,* 1966, *21,* 195-206.

Loevinger, J. *Ego development: Conceptions and theories.* San Francisco: Jossey-Bass, 1976.

Loevinger, J. *Scientific ways in the study of ego development. Vol. XII, 1978 Heinz Werner Lecture Series.* Worcester, Mass.: Clark University Press, 1979.

Loevinger, J., & Wessler, R. *Measuring ego development* (Vol. I). San Francisco: Jossey-Bass, 1970.

Loevinger, J., Wessler, R., & Redmore, C. *Measuring ego development* (Vol. 2). San Francisco: Jossey-Bass, 1970.

Mead, G.H. *Mind, self, and society.* Chicago: University of Chicago Press, 1934.

Piaget, J. *The moral judgment of the child.* Glencoe, Illinois: Free Press, 1948. (Originally published, 1932.)

Power, C. *The moral atmosphere of a just community high school; a four year longitudinal study.* Unpublished doctoral dissertation, Harvard University, 1979.

Rawls, J. *A theory of justice.* Cambridge, Mass.: Harvard University Press, 1971.

Reimer, J. A study in the moral development of kibbutz adolescents (Doctoral dissertation, Harvard University, 1977). *Dissertation Abstracts International,* 1978, *38,* 4695A. (University Microfilms No. 77-30, 695)

Rest, J. *Development in judging moral issues.* Minneapolis, Minn.: University of Minnesota Press, 1979.

Selman, R., & Jaquette, D. Stability and oscillation in interpersonal awareness. In C. Keasey (Ed.), *Nebraska Symposium on Motivation* (Vol. 25). Lincoln: University of Nebraska Press, 1977.

Sullivan, E.V., McCullough, G., & Stager, M. A developmental study of the relationship between conceptual, ego and moral development. *Child Development*, 1964, 35, 231-242.